ACKNOWLEDGEMENTS:

John Hudson, Paul Minns. Alastair Warren, Lorna Willock, Roy Woolhouse, Sally Hobson,
Markings Publications for poems by Tony Bonning and Derek Ross,
William Neill, Andrew Patterson, Daphne Brooke, Alastair Penman,
Mainstream Publishing for quote from Scottish Journey,
South West Scotland Dry Stone Walling Association for quote from Dry Stone Walling,
Alistair Barke for quote from Land of the Leal, Stuart Titles for quote from
The Silver Bough, Castle Douglas Library, Carcanet Press for the use of
material by Hugh MacDiarmid, Gavin Maxwell Enterprises Ltd for the quote
from House of Elrig, Mercat Press for quote from Exploring Scotland's Heritage Series.

Special thanks to the following for their support:
South West Scotland Screen Commission
Airds Estate
Braidwoods
Galloway Gazette
Bladnoch Distillery
Barry Smart
Ottakars Dumfries
Cally Palace & North West Castles Hotels
Rowan Glen Dairy Products
Brighouse Bay Holiday Park

Second revised edition published 2003
Copyright 1999/2003 Allan Wright & Tony Bonning

Design by Wolffe & Co., New Galloway. www.wolffeandco.com
Printed in Italy by Grafiche Milani
Digital scans by Allan Wright

ISBN 0-9536897-3-5

Published and distributed by Cauldron Press Ltd, Parton House Stables, Castle Douglas, Kirkcudbrightshire Scotland DG7 3NB
tel (+44) 1644 470260   fax (+44) 1644 470202 info@lyricalscotland.com   www.lyricalscotland.com

GALLOWAY

PHOTOGRAPHY *Allan Wright*   TEXT *Tony Bonning*

A lunky hole, designed to allow movement of sheep but not cattle between fields. Southern Upland Way, near Dalry.

INTRODUCTION

GALLOWAY mirrors Scotland as Scotland mirrors the world. Galloway has highland, lowland, farmland, river and sea. It has forest, loch, moor and mountain and it has wildlife in abundance. Galloway even has a tropical garden. It also possesses a rich and vibrant culture that is up-to-date and forward looking, yet tempered by its great past.

Galloway stretches from the River Nith to the North Channel that divides Scotland from Ireland, and from the Solway Firth to the River Stinchar. Its history predates the formation of Scotland as a sovereign nation. From its western shore stone-age man populated Ireland. From its southern shore Christianity was brought to the heathen Pict. It has been invaded by Romans, Angles, Scots and Vikings. Its people have spoken, Welsh, Latin, Anglo-Saxon, Norse and Gaelic. Even when Scotland was forged into one nation, Galloway maintained an uneasy independence.

In this book you will find the mountain wilderness of the Galloway Forest Park and its torrential rivers that descend to quiet fertile lowland. Here are peaceful woodlands set against rugged moorland, lonely cliffs and crags hammered by the sea, and beaches that change from a metre to a mile wide at the whim of the tides. Equally important, you will get a flavour of the towns, businesses, and the people's distinctive Gallovidian culture. You will also learn a little of the rich, and often savage, past that is imprinted in the stones of this land.

Here is landscape and legend, people and place, harmony and diversity. Here is GALLOWAY.

Cairnholy Chambered Cairn, above Wigtown Bay.
Designated Cairnholy 1 and the lower of the two groups of
standing stones at this site near Carsluith. The stones have
been dated at around 3000 BC.

Kirkandrews Bay, near Borgue, high summer.

The hawthorn tree forced to grow inland in an attempt to get away from the salt–laden wind blowing from the Solway shore.

The Pulhowan Burn in spate bursts through the nature reserve at the Wood of Cree.

The tower of Threave Castle, stark and forboding, transmits a sense of its own savage past.

As THE sun falls into the western ocean the high hills of Galloway rise in the strange light like muscled Titans. Shadows deepen, black defines the skyline and a million greens burn in the unearthly fire. Rivers are streams of silver as The Solway slips away from the shore leaving the land silent but for the call of the curlew.

Rain washed, mellow and muddy, the tides of the Solway have sculpted this gentle southern coast. Southwick Water and Sandyhills Bay.

A copse of Scots Pines above Knockgray on a foothill of the Cairnsmore of Carsphairn, is here set off against the soft curves of the Rhinns of Kells.

Galloway is bounded to the East by the River Nith whose estuary is easily viewed here from the summit of Criffel. The town of Dumfries is visible further up the river.

Balcary Bay looking out to Hestan Island.

SOLWAY

"The man who has never crossed the sea will never have that most beautiful sight come into his vision: the waves kissing the beaches of his homeland, gulls screaming over a harbour that he knew when young and the smoke rising from the hospitable fires of his kinsmen."

William Neill
Returning (extract)

Salmon stake nets, icons of the Solway Shore. A noisy flock of oystercatchers chase across the bay at Sandyhills.

Opposite: The sensuous fine silt of the

Solway turning gold in the sunset.

Estuary of the Urr, Kippford.

Crumbling nautical façade, Port William, 1986.

Isle of Whithorn.

Dune fence.

Blue boat, Garlieston.

Sunset across Fleet Bay, Carrick Shore.

ONE OF the fascinating peculiarities of the Solway is the range of the tide. You can paddle close by the shoreline, turn your back,

and the sea has receded anything up to a mile away. When the tide turns a brisk walk is needed to keep ahead of the incoming water.

Carsethorn, sited romantically with its toes lapping in the Solway appears to shrink beneath the Cumbrian Hills.

Gaff rigged fishing, vessel moored at Kirkcudbright, recalling a bygone era.

Southerness Lighthouse built in 1749.

The mud lined banks of the Urr here at the old port of Palnackie.

IN TIMES past the Solway Firth was a highway to the world. Two thousand years ago Galloway traded with the Middle East. It also brought invaders, most notably the Vikings, and allowed the Earls of Galloway to carry out their own marauding around the Irish Sea. One of the Solway's most famous sons was the father of the American Navy, John Paul Jones, who grew up near Southerness.

The quiet backwater of Palnackie, once a port teeming with naval trade, is now better known as the site of the World Flounder Tramping Championships, though a joyful occasion, it is a sad reflection of the decline of Galloway's great seafaring past.

The mud at low tide offers no hindrance to the working fleet at Kirkcudbright.

Garlieston, a small working harbour in the south Machars.

Drummore situated at the southern tip of the Rhinns of Galloway, is the most southerly village in Scotland.

A Sloop motoring down the Urr from Kippford, Rough Firth and Screel Hill.

FISHING IS still an important industry in the region with small fleets going out from Garlieston, Isle of Whithorn, Port William and Drummore. Kirkcudbright is Scotland's main port for shellfish, particularly scallops.

Sandyhills Bay.

The village of Rockcliffe, above, is one of the more endearing locations to be experienced on any visit to Galloway.

Working the nets at Port O'Warren, Colvend.

Impressive cliffs flank the tiny settlement at Portling on the Colvend coast. Tranquil in summer, it can also be put under seige by a turbulent Solway Firth.

Auchencairn and Balcary Bay from Bengairn.

Fleet Bay from Carrick Shore.

THE SELKIE

PERHAPS BECAUSE of its Norse past Galloway shares folklore with the Orkney and Shetland Islands. One poignant tale is that of the fisherman who took for his wife a Selkie, one of the People of the Sea. As she danced upon the shore the fisherman stole the skin that she had laid aside when she emerged from the water. Hiding the pelt in the eaves of the house he bound the maid in marriage and she bore him seven children. In all their years together she still pined for her home beneath the waves until one day her youngest child innocently revealed the whereabouts of the coat. Drawing it about herself she rushed back to the broad Solway. As the fisherman returned from his day's work he passed the Selkie who, in a melancholy voice, called to him, *"Oh man of the land I loved you, but more I loved my man of the sea."*

Lowlands and Machars

From the Nith to the North Channel there is a corridor of lowland lying between the Solway and the uplands along which now runs the A75 Euroroute.

Rising out of the Nith Valley through wood covered slopes, the countryside spreads out into farmland that would once have been open moor. Today it is almost entirely grazing pasture dedicated to raising beef cattle and sheep. The vibrant greens of the fields barely dull even in deep winter due to the warming effects of the Gulf Stream. Away to the left the granite mass of Criffel dominates the Nith estuary.

Left: Culdrain Farm near Dalbeattie takes an early summer "blessing" in style. The lush green pasture and patchwork of small forestry plantations are typical of lowland Galloway.

Opposite: the water of Dee and the Glenkens stretching up country to the Carsphairn hills, as viewed from the summit of Bengairn Hill.

"The whole appearance of the landscape changed as I reached Kirkcudbrightshire. Dumfriesshire is mainly rolling country, mounting and falling in

wide easy sweeps. But in Kirkcudbrightshire the ground is delicately varied and the small abrupt hills are broken up into little terraced shelves of green.

This interruption of all the contours arrests the eye perpetually; there are no grand effects; everything is plain and exquisite. The trees are not massed as

in Dumfriesshire but distributed singly or in little clumps as in a free and open design."

Edwin Muir
Scottish Journey (extract)

Sweetheart Abbey and Criffel.

Shambellie Wood, New Abbey.

An August sunset over an ideal location for coarse fishing near Parton on Loch Ken.

Parton village hall and the old manse shine in the clarity following a wintry rain shower.

Domestic doves beside the post box at the Old Bridge of Urr.

Crossmichael in deep midwinter. The spire of its uniquely Germanic influenced church unmistakable against the slow moving River Dee beyond.

Gatehouse of Fleet and Fleet Bay.

St Ninian's Beach, south Coast of the Machars.
The cave was where St Ninian is said to spent time in
retreat and where some relics of his presence remain.

ONCE PAST Castle Douglas, Twynholm
(birthplace of racing driver, David Coulthard)
and Gatehouse of Fleet, The heights of
Cairnsmore of Fleet force the road along the
coast. From here across Wigtown Bay can be
seen the spread of the historic Machars where
St Ninian set up his bishopric.

Twynholm, idyllic in the rolling countryside of Galloway.

The jewel of Castle Douglas, Carlingwark Loch.

Farming scene near Whauphill, the Machars.

Main street, Kirkcowan

As IF to confirm its credentials, the Machars has many religious place names: Kirkcowan, Kirkinner, Kirkchrist, Kilfillan and Glasserton to name but a few. The true beauty of this area can be best enjoyed by following the Pilgrim Way starting at either Newton Stewart or Glenluce. As the local saying goes:

"Out of the world and into Kirkcowan"

Portpatrick and a working trawler sits out a high sea running in the North Channel.

The last mile of the wonderful road journey to the Mull at the tip of the Rhinns of Galloway.

Loch Ryan resplendent under a big summer sky with Ailsa Craig or "Paddy's Milestone" and the Larne ferry.

THE EUROROUTE ends at Stranraer and Loch Ryan but the wise traveller will seek out the hammerhead peninsula known as the Rhinns of Galloway. Meaning, point or promontory, the Rhinns stretch from Milleur Point in the north to the Mull of Galloway, the most southerly tip of Scotland. The almost treeless western landscape faces the North Channel and up until recent times the town of Portpatrick was the boarding point for Ireland. The coastline is virtually one continuous cliff.

The pristine Mull of Galloway lighthouse.

The classic view of the Mull of Galloway lighthouse.

Cliffs at The Mull of Galloway

HEATHER ALE

LEGEND HAS it that the Irish king, Niall of the Nine Hostages, at the instigation of a traitor by the name Sionach, carried out a raid on a small Pictish community on the Mull of Galloway, his quest: the secret of heather ale. After a fierce battle only a father and three sons were left alive. The Picts held off the raiders until, weakened by starvation, defeat was inevitable. The eldest son Drost negotiated a surrender, saying that he would reveal the secret of the brew if, to avoid shame, Niall would slay his father and brothers. The deed done Drost said he would only reveal the secret to Sionach. Niall agreed and the last two Picts walked out of earshot to the cliff edge. Suddenly Drost threw his arms about the traitor and launched them both over the precipice, *"The secret is saved!"* he called, as they fell to their deaths.

RIVERS

Right: River Dee towards Threave Castle and Screel Hill.

Below: Creebridge over the River Cree, Newton Stewart.

Bottom right: Water of Luce and viaduct, Glenluce.

Opposite: Portpatrick, stormbound.

High and dry on the mud at Kippford where the tidal River Urr sweeps by and serves this important sailing centre.

GALLOWAY FEEDS The Solway with seven rivers: Water of Luce, Bladnoch, Cree, Water of Fleet, Dee, Urr and Nith. While the derivation of Luce and Bladnoch are in contention, Cree is almost certainly from the Gaelic *criobh*, boundary and largely seperates the Stewartry of Kirkcudbright from Wigtownshire. Fleet is the Scadinavian *fljot*, stream, while Dee would appear to correspond with Deva, the Celtic river goddess and is referred to as such by the 2nd century Roman geographer, Ptolemy. The Urr would seem to be of more ancient origin than those given by the Celts and may connect with the ancient Basque name for river, *Ur*. Ptolemy refers to the the Nith, calling it Novius which also gave the name to the Celts of Galloway, the Novantae.

Salmon still find their way up to the headwaters to spawn. In the lower reaches rivers travel through long mud lined estuaries, but as the land rises woods thicken with oak, ash, alder, birch and willow and the stone divided fields are populated by sheep. Soon, smooth streams give way to torrent and whitewater, then plantations of spruce and larch begin to dominate the landscape. A few miles on the moor begins.

Top left: the mixed land use and autumn colours lead the eye from the Black Craig (Cairnsmore of Dee) to the gentle wooded slopes leading down to the Water of Ken.

Top right: Loch Dee, surrounded by extensive conifer plantations, struggles to maintain an ecological balance. A breakthrough has been made with the introduction of an acid hardy variety of trout which provides good fishing from the loch.

Left: the Palnure Burn offers excellent fishing as it descends through the Galloway Forest Park from the foot of Cairnsmore of Fleet.

Moor and Mountain

In the time of Bruce the Galloway Forest Park was called the Forest of Buchan. The area is now largely treeless, but in bygone ages woodland covered much of today's moors and mountains and the remains of their ancient roots can still be found in upland bogs. Deforestation was most likely caused by climactic change and humankind's need for heat and shelter. The taming of fire and the discovery of the superheat properties of charcoal, making possible the smelting of iron, ensured that the settler and farmer would outlast the nomadic hunter.

Open moorland and mountain are exhilarating places to travel, with the wind chasing through purple heather and the heady scent of bog myrtle.

Deep in the remote wilderness area of the Galloway Forest Park, the Saugh Burn flows out from the foot of Merrick, the highest peak in South Scotland.

Loch Trool looking south from The Gairland Burn.

Cairnsmore of Carsphairn catching a late and low winter sun, from the ridge on Meikle Millyea, Rhinns of Kells.

The mass of the Cairnsmore of Fleet rising behind the rugged moorland above Gatehouse of Fleet.

Craignaw from Dungeon Hill, Galloway Forest Park.

Skyreburn, a perfectly formed Galloway upland glen. It rises from its own estuary just west of Gatehouse of Fleet and is a place where ecology and hill-farming seem at peace with each other.

"Scotland small? Our multiform, our infinite Scotland small?

Only as a patch of hillside may be a cliche corner

To a fool who cries 'Nothing but heather!' where in September another

Sitting there and resting and gazing round

Sees not only the heather but blaeberries

With bright green leaves and leaves already turned scarlet

Hiding ripe blue berries; and among the sage-green leaves

Of the bog-myrtle the golden flowers of the tormentil shining;

And on the small bare places, where the little Blackface sheep

Found grazing, milkworts blue as summer skies;

And down in neglected peat-hags, not worked

Within living memory, sphagnum moss in pastel shades

Of yellow, green, and pink; sundew and butterwort

Waiting with wide-open sticky leaves for their tiny winged prey;

And nodding harebells vying in their colour

With the blue butterflies that poise themselves delicately upon them;

And stunted rowans with harsh dry leaves of glorious colour.

'Nothing but heather!' - How marvelously descriptive! And incomplete!"

Hugh MacDiarmid
Direadh (extract)

Loch Enoch

BATTLE OF THE BOULDERS

A STRANGE anomaly is the presence of Granite boulders on the top of Merrick. The area has a preponderance of erratic boulders and legend has it that the cause was a dispute between the great god Pan and His Satanic Majesty, the Devil. Each with their armies fought a merciless battle across the Gallovidian ranges. After three days and nights only Pan and the Devil were left alive. Aching with hunger and only one loaf between them, (now petrified on top of Craignaw), they agreed to a competition of bowls on the flat surface of Wee Craignaw, now called the Devil's Bowling Green. The result was unsatisfactory and the battle resumed using boulders torn from the mountainsides until the landscape was littered. Deciding it was better to fight another day Pan retreated and the Devil was left to consume the loaf. Having cut only one slice, Satan was instantly struck dead by a bolt of lightening cast by Pan's father, Jupiter. And so ended the Battle of the Boulders.

The Devil's Bowling Green on the west side of Craignaw is a mysterious place to encounter.

The derelict remains of a croft at the site of the disused lead mine beneath the Black Gairy at Carsphairn.

Corserine Hill and wintering geese near Balmaghie.

Glacial boulders lie still in the Nick of the Dungeon.

GALLOWAY IS superb walking country, and none better can be found than in the Galloway Forest Park. Standing on the bare granite top of Craignaw the climber is surrounded by mountains: northwards, the Dungeon and Mullwharcher, eastwards, the range of the Rhinns of Kells with the peaks of Meaul, Millfire and Corserine; to the south, the heights of Lairg and Lamachan; and to the west, Benyellary and The Merrick.

Forest

Two WORLD wars drew heavily on Britain's timber resources and as a result, in the late forties and early fifties, the government set about a major program of forestation.

Now the forestry authorities recognise the need for ecological balance and are replacing large areas of felled softwood with native hardwood.

A rich tapestry of colour and texture is offered in the depths of a mature, mixed forest environment such as here at Shambellie Wood near New Abbey.

From Dungeon Hill looking down on "pre-enlightenment plantation" across the Silver Flow and Loch Dungeon to the Rhinns of Kells, Galloway Forest Park.

A majestic oak gives shade to spring lambs, Upper Nithsdale.

Spring prepares to explode in the climax woodland of Castramon Nature Reserve near Gatehouse of Fleet.

"Pit back the aik, the rowan and the sally

see yince again the blackthorn on the druim;

rowan an elm, the birk and bonie gean

for as our roots haud tae yir native yird

sae mankind staunds,

an as we faa tae nocht sae mankind faas

an the hail mapamound

crines tae a steirless craig withooten saul,

whaur the suin's licht

faas on the beildless stour o a beld stern"

William Neill
Tree Speik (extract)

on the foothills around Cairnsmore of Fleet the scattered remains of the native birch wood.

"Put back the oak, the rowan and the willow

see again the blackthorn on the hill;

rowan and elm, the birch and wild cherry

for as our roots hold to our native earth

so mankind stands

and as we fall to nothing so mankind falls

and the whole sphere of the world

withers to a silent soulless rock

where the sun's light

falls on the dust of a naked star."

Translation
Tony Bonning

ROCK AND STONE

THE GREATER part of Galloway is divided almost
equally between Ordovician and Silurian shales and
greywackes in a roughly north west and south east
formation. There is a significant formation of
sandstone around Stranraer and three major granite
formations at Craignaw, Cairnsmore of Fleet and
Criffel. Granite is quarried at Creetown and
Dalbeattie, and stone from the latter was used in the
construction of the Thames Embankment and the
Bank of England.

Stone has been used as a building material in
Galloway for at least five thousand years. Neolithic
peoples built chambered tombs across the region,
the most famous being Cairnholy near Creetown.
Others can be found at Boreland, Dranandow,
Cairnderry and Bargrennan in the Stewartry and at
Cairnscarrow, Mid Gleniron, High Gillespie and the
Caves of Kilhern in Wigtownshire.

cup and ring marks preserved at Drumtroddan in the Machars.

the monumental Cairnholy 2 stones.

an imposing stone at Garplefoot between New Galloway and Dalry stands bold in the winter sunshine.

the scattered stone remains of Polmaddie village which is now a recognised heritage site at Dundeugh, North Glenkens.

CUP AND ring markings are a feature of Galloway stone-age culture that unites this country with the rest of the ancient world. These enigmatic designs are found in Australia, South America, China, the Pacific Islands, Russia and South Africa. As to their meaning: there are well over one hundred explanations.

Galloway's cairns, standing stones and stone circles, though not on the scale of Stonehenge or Callanish, are impressive, and a visitor to Torhousie near Wigtown will not be disappointed.

Probably the most famous of these structures is the Carlin's Cairn sitting atop Corserine Hill. It is fifty five feet in diameter and stands at a height of ten feet. The name Carlin, though often thought of as witch, is in fact the Norse word for a woman. The cairn is reputed to have been built by Robert the Bruce in commemoration of an old woman at nearby Craigencallie who gave him refuge. Another tale says that it was a miller's wife at Polmaddie who built the cairn in memory of Robert the Bruce.

CASTLE AND KEEP

DEFENSIVE STRUCTURES in early Galloway were either hillforts or crannogs. The latter were artificial islands built from trees weighed down with boulders. On top a large wood and thatch roundhouse was built.

The arrival of the Normans in the twelfth century saw the construction of mottes: timber buildings set atop an artificial mound and surrounded by a stockade. The buildings were later coated with clay as a defence against attack by fire.

The following centuries saw these wooden structures replaced by stone and were the prototypes of the great thirteenth century castles.

On Carlingwark Loch, by Castle Douglas three, willow covered islets at one time supported ancient dwellings or crannogs.

The Romano Iron Age settlement at Clatteringshaws Loch.

THERE ARE many mottes in the Stewartry and
Wigtownshire. The most significant of these is the
Motte of Urr:

*"Covering an area of about two hectares, this truly impressive
earthwork is the most extensive motte and bailey castle in Scotland.
Only perhaps from the air can one appreciate its great size, looking
for all the world like some earthen battleship stranded on the alluvial
river plain. Its position in the valley is not especially commanding;
it may originally have been an island, but the river now flows in a
single channel to the east. Close up, its deep outer ditch puts one in
mind of an iron-age hillfort, and it is possible that the bailey was
developed out of an existing fortification in Anglo-Norman times."*

Geoffrey Stell
Exploring Scotland's Heritage
(Mercat Press)

The Motte of Urr.

Castle Kennedy

Old Place of Mochrum

Orchardton

Cardoness

ALTHOUGH LARGE numbers of castles are now reduced to mere heaps of rubble, there are more than enough impressive structures to satisfy the curious. The majority are no-nonsense towers of stone, built, not for decoration, but for defence: Carsluith, Castle Kennedy, Castle of Park, Old Place of Mochrum and Stranraer in Wigtownshire and Cardoness, Orchardton and Threave in Kirkcudbrightshire are among the most impressive. Orchardton, near Auchencairn, is the only round tower in Scotland. Buittle, now gone, though being excavated, was twice the royal court of the Baliol family in 1293 and 1332. Threave was the seat of the Douglas family, their lands granted to them for services to Robert the Bruce in the Wars of Independence. Threave was built around 1370 by the Third Earl, Archibald The Grim.

Loch Doon Castle moved and rebuilt around 1935 from its island site stone by stone in order to accommodate the practicalities of the Galloway Hydro Scheme.

Dunskey Castle precipitously perched on the cliffs by Portpatrick.

Threave Castle sunset in the grip of winter.

The classic view of the town of Kirkcudbright from the bridge showing 16th century architecture juxtaposed with the working harbour.

The preserved remains of McClellan's Castle which dominates the broad vista along St Cuthbert St.

ANCIENT
GALLOWAY

"Our history,

tidal as the Solway

is washed up on

these bays and estuaries.

A library

that requires

only our time

and inclination

to pause, and browse."

a lilac sunset descends upon the lower stones at Cairnholy.

"Scattered here and there,
revealed at low tide,
the nets and poles
of stake nets,
are the webs and spines
of old books
and the rush of the sea
seems but the ruffle
of our pages."

Derek Ross

Salmon stake nets at the The Inks, Creetown.

Timelessness is suggested here on the banks of Loch Ken.

THE GALLOWAY of six thousand years ago was a savage land where a few small tribes of hunter-gatherers, adept in the uses of stone, survived on the fringe of land along the shoreline of Luce Bay. The entire population of Scotland is believed to have measured in the hundreds.

A thousand years later, migrating tribes of hunters entered the almost impenetrable forest that covered all but the highest of the mountains. They passed beneath giant oaks, almost five metres in girth, hacked their way through thickets of willow, hazel and alder, before breaking out on to the pine covered slopes of the interior. On the way they encountered bears, wild pig and wild ox, and out on the open moor, elk, wolf and reindeer.

Monreith Beach overlooking Luce Bay on the south west coast of the Wigtownshire Machars.

A catchy title might be "The Wigtownshire Ploughman" were it not for the fact that the farmer is not ploughing but ridging, on the Rhinns of Galloway.

A THOUSAND years later a pastoral people cleared the flatlands beside the rivers and began farming:

a process that would bring about the demise of the great forests and much of its divergent wildlife.

THE CELTS

Two THOUSAND years on, Galloway was populated by the Celts. In these times the Solway was a crossroads of sea travel to other lands and the people traded with Ireland, Southern England, France and the Mediterranean. After the Roman invasion of 49 A.D., and their arrival in Galloway in 82 A.D., the tribes preserved an uneasy truce until the retreat of the Romans behind Hadrian's Wall two hundred years later.

Ptolemy's map of Scotland shows Galloway as having two main centres: Lycopibia and Rerigonium. The former is possibly present day Whithorn and the latter, translating through the Celtic language, as Cairnryan.

Whithorn, the site of *Candida Casa*, the White House, (Anglo-Saxon, *hwit erne*), is the oldest inhabited town in Scotland. It is the birthplace of Christianity north of Hadrian's Wall and a centre of pilgrimage for kings and commoners for a thousand years. It was from here that St Ninian set out to convert the Southern Picts.

The ruin of St Ninian's Priory is at the Whithorn archeological site.

The High Street of Whithorn has an impressive breadth and character.

Mochrum Loch, deep in the Machars, appears ancient cold and mysterious.

Range of the Awful Hand, Galloway Forest Park.

The Colvend Coast from the summit of Criffel as it would have appeared to the raiding Northmen in ancient times.

ANGLES, SCOTS AND NORSEMEN

IN TIME, the Brythonic, Welsh speaking people of Galloway were overun by the warlike Teutonic tribes of Nordhymbraland, Northumberland. Though Anglo-Saxon and Briton fought merciless battles over the centuries, invasion was not necessarily always a bloodthirsty affair. Christianity was, by that time, a uniting force; not to mention the exchange of trade and technology. By the eighth century Whithorn was an Anglian Bishopric.

The land saw no rest from invaders: in 841 A.D. the Scots under Alpin, father of the Scottish king Kenneth MacAlpin, raided deep into Galloway. It cost him dearly: he was shot by an arrow near Loch Ryan. In 866 A.D. Viking longships began to harass Gallovidian coastal settlements. In time these fierce and intrepid sea raiders settled across the region and, like others before them, left an indelible mark.

By the Eleventh century the kingdom of the Scots covered much of what is now modern Scotland, with the exception of Galloway. Somehow, through all its adversity, it maintained a singular identity. Perhaps the topography of the land combined with the legendary wildness of its people kept it in isolation. Even the name Galloway has persisted for fifteen hundred years: a rare feat for a land that has seen so many invasions.

The rugged mass of Cairnharrow rising unexpectedly above the wintery moorland behind Gatehouse of Fleet.

The first major Galwegian ruler to appear in the history books is Fergus of Galloway (c. 1120-60). In his attempts to maintain Galloway's independence, Fergus joined forces with the Scottish king, David the First, in his foray over the border in 1137-8. This culminated in the Battle of the Standard. Though armed only with a small shield and short throwing spear, the Gallovidians claimed their right to be the vanguard of the army. Their renowned savagery was no match for bowmen and armoured Anglo-Norman chivalry:

"The Gallovidians attacked with such force that the Northumbrian front line of spearmen had to give ground 'but they (the Gallovidians) were driven off again by the strength of the knights' who were impenetrable as a wall of iron. While held against that wall, Gallovidians took the brunt of the archers' deadly accuracy. Their berserkers fought on oblivious of wounds, each 'like a hedgehog with its quills...bristling all round with arrows and nonetheless brandishing his sword, and in blind madness rushing forward'."

Daphne Brooke
Wild Men and Holy Places

Loch Valley may have an unoriginal name but is a wild and remote place deep in the Galloway Highlands.

Ross Bay an idyllic location nestling at the estuary of the River Dee.

Clatteringshaws Loch.

AFTER THE death of Fergus in 1161, Norman influence was felt across Scotland and Galloway. The first motte and bailey castles were erected and feudalism introduced. At this time Nithsdale and Carrick ceased to be part of the region and the present boundaries were established. Fergus's great grandson, Alan, is thought of as the last king of Galloway. Alan had no son and his three daughters married Anglo-Norman barons who were more concerned in keeping favour with the English king, Edward the First. Effectively, Galloway became a vassal province of England and at the Battle of Bannockburn in 1314, Galloway troops, who always claimed the vanguard of the Scottish army, were conspicuously absent.

Bruce and the Douglases

"A! fredome is a noble thing!

Fredome mayss man to haiff liking;

Fredom all solace to man giffis:

He levys at ess that frely levys!

A noble hart may haiff nane ess

Na ellys nocht that may him pless

Gyff fredome failyhe: for fre liking

Is yharnyt our all other thing."

ess, ease; ellys, ills; failyhe, fail;
yharnyt, yearned.

John Barbour (1320-1395)
The Brus

Loch Trool, opposite the site of the famous victory over the English in 1307.

ALTHOUGH IN the early part of his career Robert the Bruce won important battles in Galloway, at Raploch Moss and Glentrool, he was no welcome visitor. During his time as a fugutive in the Galloway mountains he was persistently harassed by the MacDoualls of Wigtownshire. In time Bruce would have his revenge and declare his brother, Edward, Lord of Galloway.

Edward Bruce's tenure was short-lived, and in the years following the death of Robert the Bruce in 1332, part of Galloway once more came under English suzerainty. This would last until 1369 when Archibald Douglas, son of Robert Bruce's right hand man, James, the Black Douglas, was made Earl of Galloway. Archibald forged the region into a single unit and indelibly linked the names of Douglas with Galloway.

CHURCH AND STATE

In 1560 the Scottish Parliament abolished the authority of the Pope and effectively established the Presbyterian Church of Scotland.

Later, in the seventeenth century, this led to the *Killing Times*, which swept across Galloway, when supporters of the National Covenant, signed in 1638, were mercilessly persecuted. The most famous covenanters were the Wigtown Martyrs: Margaret Wilson and Margaret McLachlan, who, in May of 1658, were put to death by being tied to stakes before the incoming tide.

The commemorative stone erected in Wigtown Bay scene of the famous Wigtown martyrs' deaths.

Opposite: Off season, at Threave Castle.

The Agricultural Revolution

Upland summer pasture Rhinns of Kells near New Galloway.

Though the process of transforming Galloway through farming began some four thousand years ago the real transformation began in earnest in the early eighteenth century:

"Dry stane dyking, in a comprehensive way, was first undertaken on the lands of Palgown in the west of the Stewartry of Kirkcudbright. Somewhere about 1710, when the early Enclosure Acts were passed, the brothers McKie leased pieces of land free to people who would work for them in the summer.

In the spring, these people took to the hills with tents of sorts, and poles. In a very few days they had built themselves huts of turf and stone. Heather thatched the roofs and heather made their beds. The huts can have differed very little from the shielings to which Highlanders migrated every year on the first of May, for the summer grazing. The brothers McKie were their own foremen, and in a year or two many square miles of otherwise useless land were enclosed by dry stane dykes, fine strong erections, and the value of the McKie's lands was increased at least fourfold."

F. Rainsford-Hannay
Dry Stone Walling

Meandering between the Saugh Burn and Loch Enoch in the Galloway Highlands runs this superbly ruined dyke. Described by Alastair Warren (hillwalker & former editor of the local newspaper) as "The Oldest Dyke in Creation".

Restored dyke and habitat-rich, wilder pasture. Current, ecologically sensitive farming schemes encourage the protection of such resources, Grobdale of Balmaghie.

The traditional dry stane dyke. Its "texture", is highly compatible with the Galloway landscape.

Farmers relaxing at the Carsphairn Show,
a traditional hill country venue for
Blackface sheep and rural crafts.

Remote farm cottage at Clenrie on the Southern
Upland Way.

Nether Laggan farm, Parton

Prime livestock raised on the banks of the
River Dee by Crossmichael. Beef is a valuable
commodity in the Galloway Economy

Farm signs in Galloway express a way of life.

LANGUAGE

THE MANY languages that have been spoken in Galloway are recorded in local place names:

Bonnie, bonnie Gallowa': and those spots in the Rhinns dearest above all.

Allandoo, Achgammie, Achneel, Auchnotteroch, Auchterlinachan, Auchtrimakain, Ardwell Bay, Auchness, Auchlea, Auchneight;

Balscalloch, Barnhills, Barnscarroch, Bughtpark, Balwhinie, Barbeth, Balgown, Barscarrow, Barncorkerie, Barnchalloch;

Cairnbrook, Cairnhandy, Cairngarroch, Cairnwellan, Cairnbowie, Craigmodie, Craigencrosh, Craigcaffey, Corsewell, Carrickadoyn, Clachan Heughs, Colfin, Culchintie, Currochtrie, Clachanmore, Culgroat, Clayshant, Clanyard, Crummag, Cardrain, Cardoyne, Chapel Rossan, Clipper Drigan Well;

Dunanrea, Drummore, Dumbreddan, Dinduff, Dindinnie, Dinvin, Dunman, Damnaglaur, Drumantrae, Dundream, Drumfad, Dundribban;

Enoch;

Fintlock;

Genoch, Glengyre, Glengitter, Glenstockadle, Grennan, Garrochtrie, Glenoch, Gachvie Moss, Gladenoch,;

High Mark, High Maggarty;

Knocknain, Knockneen, Knockcoid, Knockieausk, Knockmudloch, Kirkminnoch, Kirklaughlane, Kirkmagill, Kirkmadrine, Kildonan, Killumpha;

Lochans, Lagvag, Lagganmore;

Mull of Logan, Mulldaddie, Marslaugh, Myroch, Muntloch, Meikle Gladnoch;

Nick o' Kindrum;

Pirnminnoch, Portlogan, Portayew, Portpatrick, Portencalzie, Portcarvillan, Portnaighton, Portencorkerie;

Ringvinachan, Ringuinea;

Slunkrainey, Slouchnawen, Sandell Bay, Sandhead;

Tarbet, Tandoo, Terally;

West Freuch.

James Barke

Land of the Leal

Stranraer, Loch Ryan and the Larne Ferry.

Towns

Two THOUSAND years ago Galloway had two towns. Two hundred years ago there were little more, and what few there were would, today, be classified as villages. The last two centuries have seen a gradual change from a pastoral to an urban existence and the consequent growth of townships. Gallovidian towns are comparatively small and agreeable places to live. Castle Douglas, Gatehouse of Fleet and Newton Stewart are relatively modern, being built in the mid-nineteenth century. Stranraer as a major ferry port is a recent creation, with services to Larne beginning in October 1862.

The county towns of Kirkcudbright and Wigtown are Anglian settlements from Medieval times. The name of the former means the Church of Cuthbert, from the Old English spelling of his name, *Cudbriht*. The latter is possibly a combination of *wic*, Norse for a settlement in a bay, and *ton*, Anglo-Saxon for a settlement: or Towntown - a not-uncommon quirk when the language of the invader overlays the native tongue.

Opposite: Kirkcudbright from The Stell.

The impressive Wigtown County Buildings. The town is experience a renaissance through its new status as Scotland's Booktown.

St John's Town of Dalry nestling in the Glenkens, behind it rises the mass of the Carsphairn Hills.

The bandstand, Colliston Park, Dalbeattie.

In Stone Age Galloway it is likely that everyone was, to a greater or lesser degree, adept in what we call craft. The ability to fabricate weapons, boats, baskets and dwellings was directly related to survival in an uncompromising world.
The first evidence of art in the region is carved in stone. These are the cup and ring markings which probably date from as far back as 3000 BC.

It was not until the early medieval period that art on any scale began to flourish: the subject matter was almost entirely religious. Later, the great Gallovidian abbeys would stand as a testament to the skills of those artists and craft workers.

One of the more recent centres of art in the region is Kirkcudbright, home of Jessie M. King and A.E. Hornel both nationally renowned early 20th century artists.

Since the 1960's Galloway has attracted artists and craftspeople of all persuasions. There is a thriving literary scene, numerous art galleries, glassblowers, painters, potters, wood carvers and some of the finest weavers of willow in Scotland.

Two substantial stones remain at Drumtroddan in the Machars.

Cistercian monks once inhabited what is now the graceful ruin of Dundrennan Abbey, located on the quiet coast road

between Kirkcudbright and Auchencairn.

Kirkcudbright harbour, 1984.

MYTH, LEGEND AND FOLKLORE

THE STORIES of St Ninian are among Galloway's great contribution to legend. In the matter of folklore and folktales Galloway has a rich abundance.

A witchy moon rises in the twilight, Kirkgunzeon.

Tourhouskie Stone Circle in The Machars is an impressive example of a site of ancient ritual.

The "auld brig" at Kendoon village next to a place where in the seventeenth century, a tinkler, suspected of theft, was chased by a troop of dragoons. They drove him towards a ravine on the River Deugh, and, with a final cry of triumph, descended on their prey. In an act that combined desperation with bravery, the tinkler leaped and cleared the chasm. Since that time the place has been named The Tinkler's Loup.

River Bladnoch and the Distillery.

Wigtown Harbour.

THE BROWNIE OF BLEDNOCH

DRESSED IN nothing more than a kilt of rushes a spectral figure enters the farm-town at dusk. People draw back in horror at the unearthly sight: his gash of a mouth, a nose no more than a hole and a terrifying glint in his eye. In a mumble he asks for work. This creates near hysteria until the farm owner pulls out a Bible and commands him to say where he has come from. The brownie tells of living by a stream in a land with no sky, but that he will now live in the farm-town if they will but give him work. The young women protest until the farmer's wife realises, that with not enough workers to bring in the late harvest, the brownie's services will help prevent disaster. And so Aiken-drum sets to work cutting the corn, gathering in the sheep at night and singing lullabies to the children: and all for a mere bowl of milk. Every wish is granted and soon he is an accepted part of the community. All is well until a young woman, new-married into the farm-town and offended by the near nakedness of the brownie, lays an old pair of trousers by his bowl of milk. To the mind of Aiken-drum this is a wage and the signal that his services are no longer required: and so he leaves. Long afterwards his wailing lamentations are heard across the countryside and those who had previously feared his presence now regret his passing.

"There cam a strange wight to out town-en'
And the fient a body did him ken
He tirled na lang, but he glided ben
Wi' a dreary dreary hum"

wight, supernatural being; tirled, knocked; ben, easily;

From The Brownie of Blednoch by William Nicholson
(1738-1849) born in Borgue and buried at Kirkandrews

Vernacular style Galloway cottage by the Dhoon, Kirkcudbright Bay.

CUSTOM

THE RAPID introduction of motor cars and television after World War Two accelerated the demise of specifically local customs and festivities. Isolation had kept them alive for centuries and in a few decades they were gone. Fifty years ago in Galloway Christmas was just another day. Hogmanay, December 31st, was the time for almost Bacchanalian festivities:

"In Galloway (Minnigaff 1895) the foreman used to enter the farmer's bedroom as first foot carrying with him a sheaf and a bottle of whisky. He cast the sheaf over the farmer and his wife, then poured out the whisky, including a glass for himself, and drank the good health to the family and prosperity to the farm."

The Silver Bough Vol 1
F. Marian McNeill

Variations on this custom were carried on throughout Galloway. The custom of carrying a turnip lantern at Halloween is perhaps a reminder of something more sinister:

"The turnip lantern is probably the last surviving symbol connected with the Celtic Cult of the Severed Head which used to meet on Carlingwark Hill at Castle Douglas in Kirkcudbrightshire, where ritual sacrifice once took place. There the local Druid would remove the head from a victim and ritually bind it with cords and it would then be given the place of honour at future celebrations."

Some Customs, Folklore and Superstitions of Galloway
Alastair Penman

The Cree in spate passes under the fine Granite construction of the Creebridge at Newton Stewart.

PLANT LORE

THOUGH ROUGHLY on the same latitude as Moscow and Hudson's Bay, Galloway enjoys a temperate climate. This is due to the influence of the Gulf Stream bringing warm waters from the Gulf of Mexico.

Spring growth is luxurious and the region is rich in wild flowers and plants. Travel the winding back roads and you will pass through avenues of hawthorn, wild rose, elderflower and honeysuckle. Later in the season the verges are thick with foxglove, red campion and rosebay willowherb. Pause for a moment in cool woodlands and you will see among the carpet of mosses and fern: sorrel, violet and anemone, speedwell, pimpernell, self heal and bugle flower.

Like moor and mountain the seeming plainness of the bogs belies the wealth of plant life that lies among rush and grass.

Brighouse Bay is the location of the rare Blue Flax.

August and Galloway is ablaze with Rosebay Willowherb.

Wild orchids proliferate in the wet meadowlands of wild Galloway.

Foxgloves are abundant among the conifers.

The fabulous summer herbaceous border laid out to great effect in front of Threave House. Owned by the National Trust for Scotland and opened to the public in 1949, Threave Garden is one of the most visited sites in the whole region.

Over-wintering Greylag geese graze at the foot of Screel Hill.

Visit any of Galloway's open gardens and one soon becomes aware of the abundance of bird life: Galloway is renowned for bird-watching. Wintering wildfowl on the Solway is an obvious attraction, but the many rivers, lochs, wetlands, woods and forests offer a wealth of species. There are thirty recognised ornithological sites in the region.

You will find in Galloway; the flycatcher, redstart, warbler, whitethroat and water rail. On Wigtown Bay breed wader, duck and tern. In the Galloway Forest Park are siskin, crossbill, wagtail, dipper and nightjar. Fleet Oakwoods offer woodpecker, jay and woodcock. Further east at Rockcliffe are greenshank, ringed plover, cormorant and rock pipit.

The adventurous walker who tackles the *Southern Upland Way* can see skylark, meadow pipit, short-eared owl, raven, kestrel, merlin and buzzard, and at certain times even the hen harrier, osprey and golden eagle.

Young Barn Owls discovered as fledglings in the kitchen of an abandoned farmhouse near Grobdale. The nest was in a loft space above but by good fortune the young birds had the entire space of the kitchen as a nursery to learn to fly in.

Southern Upland Way

The Southern Upland Way, which runs from Portpatrick on the West Coast to Cockburnspath on the East Coast of Scotland, takes in the best that Galloway has to offer. Started in 1984, the Way is 340km (202 miles) long, and the trek would take the average walker about two weeks to cover: the Galloway section from Portpatrick to Sanquhar takes four or five days. The route goes by Stranraer, Castle Kennedy, Bargrennan, Glen Trool, Clatteringshaws, Dalry and Benbrack, and is seen as the hardest part of the journey.

Witch's Rock on the coastal path at the start of the Southern Upland Way near Portpatrick.

Harsh March light flickers across reeds and hillside by Caldons, near the south end of Loch Trool, Southern Upland Way.

Blawquairn Farm, Dalry, Southern Upland Way.

Sunset over Carsfad Loch, Upper Glenkens

WILD ANIMALS

Feral Goat, Galloway Forest Park

RED DEER became extinct in the mid 18th century, but today a reserve in the Galloway Forest Park contains a large herd reintroduced during the 19th century. Roe Deer are also found in the woodlands.

The most memorable of all the region's wildlife has to be the mountain goat. These great-horned, shaggy-coated beasts can be found all across the hills of Galloway. Reputed to be domesticated animals gone feral during the clearances of the early 19th century, the wild goat is now an icon of the Galloway Forest Park.

Foxes are common, and the species found here are larger than their southern counterparts. On lower ground the dedicated naturalist can find badgers and related species like the stoat, weasel, and the shy pine marten. Both mountain hare and brown hare are still in good numbers, as are the otter and the red squirrel. The observant walker will find field mice, voles, shrews, adders, newts, lizards, frogs and toads. Certain foreign mammals like sika deer and mink have established themselves across the country and, despite destabilising the ecosystem, will inevitably be accepted as part of it.

Young Roe Deer, Wood of Cree.

Red Deer Stags, Galloway Forest Park

LIVESTOCK ANCIENT AND MODERN

BEFORE THE Enclosure Acts of the early 18th century and the creation or growth of the region's towns, the countryside was well populated and most people owned goats, sheep and, perhaps, a cow. The goats would have been little different from the wild goats of today, the sheep little different from black-faced hill sheep and the cattle, small, rough-coated and sturdy. The province was famous for horses.

Know we not Galloway nags?

William Shakespeare
King Henry IV Part II

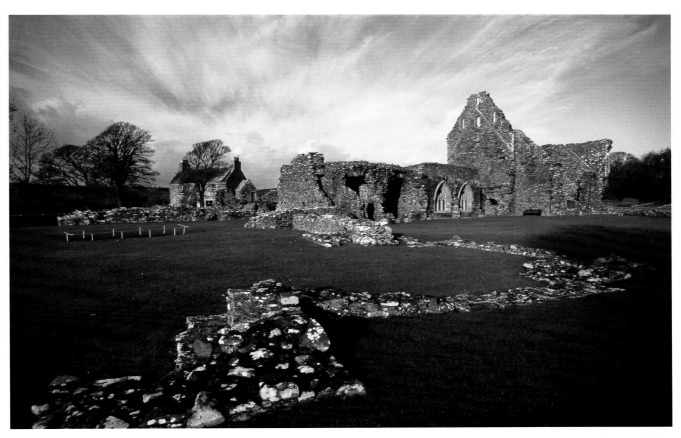

Glenluce Abbey.

These horses were highly rated as they had a unique ability to negotiate mountain, moor and bog. It is said to have been a Galloway horse that Bruce rode at Bannockburn in 1314 when he defeated the English champion, Walter deBohun, in single combat.

The breed is now extinct, but was probably brought by the Norse invaders and shared a common ancestry with the Icelandic and Highland ponies of today.

Cistercian monks at Dundrennan, Sweetheart and Glenluce developed successful sheep farms.

A gathering of young blackface sheep on the crispest of winter mornings in the Glenkens.

Trio on the hill.

Intense scrutiny from the tweed caps, Blackface judging, Carsphairn Show.

By the shores of Loch Doon, blackface sheep sillouetted against the twin peaks of Coran of Portmark
and Black Craig, north end of the Rhinns of Kells, Galloway Forest Park.

SHEEP CONTINUE to proliferate in Galloway and
the blackface is still found on the hill. On the
lowland they are now mainly cross-bred Leicester
ewes, Scotch Mules and Texels.

A black Galloway cow poses by a vernacular Galloway farmhouse complete with dry Stane dyke, Nether Rusko, Water of Fleet.

THE ENCLOSURE acts of the 18th century had the effect of improving the quality of pasture, which in turn led to better quality of sheep and cattle. This, and the opening up of the English markets through the Union of Parliaments in 1707, turned cattle droving into a major industry. The distinctive black Galloway cattle were then driven in their thousands to the fattening pastures of Norfolk.

"The true Galloway breed of cattle, in proportion to their size, is the handsomest and best in Britain and draws the best price in every market in the kingdom."

Statistical Account 1795

Hereford cow grazes by a hawthorn tree, near Laurieston.

IN TIME there was a gradual replacement of the Galloway cow with the Ayrshire as a dairy economy developed. The Ayrshire in its turn was replaced by the higher volume Friesian and Holstein. From World War Two beef production increased and saw the return of the Galloway; though more recently, continental crosses such as Charolais, Simmental and Limousin are the major strains.

Perhaps the most readily identifiable breed is the Belted Galloway. Hornless and black with a broad white cummerbund, the Beltie is one of Galloway's most endearing and enduring symbols.

Two belted Galloway bulls tête a tête.

The River Cree and Cairnsmore of Fleet in the distance.

Gallovidians Ancient and Modern

Galloway has many famous sons and daughters The earliest recorded people were the 1st century Novantae, but no singular name has come down from that period. It is not until the 5th century that a specific name appears: that of Ninian, the Roman educated Briton and Christian saint.

Better known in his time, at least for those who lived to tell the tale, was the great 11th century Norse leader, Thorfinn Skullsplitter, who held nine earldoms, including Galloway.

"Earl Thorfinn dwelt for the most part.......at the place called Gaddgedlar where Scotland and England meet."
The Orkneyinga Saga, (14th century)

Gaddgedlar, is thought to be a Norse corruption of Galwydia, Galloway.

On his death his allegedly Galwegian wife, Ingibiorg, married Malcolm Canmore, son of King Duncan, who was famously murdered by Macbeth. This marriage united most of the whole of present day Scotland.

Though Galloway was renowned for its wild men, it is equally renowned for having produced one of history's kindest hearts: Devorgilla. The wife of John Baliol, she is responsible for the setting up of Baliol college at Oxford in the 13th century. She also founded monasteries for the Black Friars in Wigtown and the Grey Friars in Dumfries who specialised in caring for the sick and poor, and arranged the building of a stone bridge across the River Nith, which still stands to this day. Her most significant local monument is Sweetheart Abbey near the Nith estuary.

Though history tends to recount the tales of those of royal blood, 18th century Galloway had its own Gypsy sovereign, Billy Marshall, King of the Randies. Reputed to have lived to the age of 120, Billy led the Levellers in the fight against the enclosures. He is also said to have attended the historic Keltonhill Fair for over a hundred years, even deserting the Royal Regiment of Dragoons in Flanders to honour the tryst.

Though now berated for his florid prose style, the nineteenth century Gallovidian novelist Samuel Rutherford Crocket, was enormously popular in his time. His most famous book, The Raiders, is still in print and first editions are sought by collectors.

Hestan Island from Balcary Bay, featured in S.R. Crocket's novel "The Raiders".

Sweetheart Abbey.

Ruined dyke on Benyellary, Galloway Forest Park.

River Dee opposite the hamlet of Balmaghie, deep in the Stewartry. A landscape perhaps little changed from the days

of Billy Marshall, and near the scene of the Keltonhill Fair.

Parton Church, site of the burial place of James Clerk Maxwell.

The bronze otter perched high above Monreith Bay in the Machars was created to commemorate the life of Gavin Maxwell.

RATED BY Einstein as probably the greatest ever scientist, James Clerk Maxwell has deep associations with Galloway. Without his pioneering work it is unlikely that physics would have progressed as it did. He is buried at Parton Cemetery.

Lesser known in his own country, the Whithorn born Alistair Reid is a writer and poet of international class and reputation. Resident in Manhattan he regularly contributes to the *New Yorker.*

The village of Minnigaff, now absorbed into Newton Stewart, has much to be proud of having associations with two giants in the academic filed:

Alexander Murray was born in 1775 at Dunkitterick under the shadow of Cairnsmore of Fleet. The son of a shepherd, he attended Minnigaff school, and, by the age of seventeen, was conversant in French, Latin, Greek, Hebrew, Anglo Saxon, Welsh and Arabic. Though dying at thirty-seven, he became professor of Oriental Languages at Edinburgh University.

One hundred and sixty years later, in 1936, Minnigaff was the birthplace of a modern day genius: Sir James Alexander Mirrlees, economist and Nobel Laureate. Educated at Douglas-Ewart High School in Newton Stewart, he later became an economics professor at both Oxford and Cambridge, winning the Nobel Prize in 1996.

Along with MacDouall and Douglas, the other great family name of Galloway is Maxwell. The power of the Maxwells was first assumed in the region after the fall of the Douglases in the 15th century. In recent times the Maxwell family has produced two great writers. The first is Sir Herbert Maxwell, prolific writer and chronicler of all things Gallovidian; the other is his grandson, Gavin, author of many fine books, but best known for *Ring of Bright Water*. Born in the Machars, Gavin Maxwell has written the great Gallovidian eulogy, *The House of Elrig:*

Heather moorland at the foot of Merrick, Galloway Highlands

"John and I explored the kingdom from which I had been exiled for so long, the high, wind-whining moorlands of rock and heather, the far hill and sea horizons; and in his company I consolidated a long-lost position. We went to look for an eagle's nest in the Galloway Hills, and as we scrambled up the rain-gleaming rock and scree I asked, because this was important, 'John, what do you ordinarily do in the holidays?' he said: 'Well, nothing as good as this,' and suddenly the rock and the rain and all the gigantic windswept kingdom of Galloway seemed mine to live in, all exile over."

Feral goats, Dungeon Hill.

THE END